WHAT'S IN YOUR CHICKEN NUGGET?

Jaclyn Sullivan

PowerKiDS press™

New York

To all the kids who eat their vegetables

Published in 2012 by The Rosen Publishing Group, Inc.
29 East 21st Street, New York, NY 10010

First Edition

Editor: Sara Antill
Book Design: Greg Tucker

Photo Credits: Cover, pp. 4, 16 Comstock/Thinkstock; pp. 5, 7 (top), 9 (top), 13, 14, 15, 19 (left), 22 Shutterstock.com; p. 6 Paul Prescott/Shutterstock.com; p. 8 Stockbyte/Thinkstock; p. 9 (bottom) Jupiterimages/Photos.com/Thinkstock; pp. 10, 12 © 2011 The Associated Press; p. 11 Jupiterimages/ Comstock/Thinkstock; p. 17 © www.iStockphoto.com/Laura Eisenberg; p. 18 Foodcollection/Getty Images; p. 19 (top) BananaStock/Thinkstock; p. 21 Jack Hollingsworth/Digital Vision/Thinkstock.

Library of Congress Cataloging-in-Publication Data

Sullivan, Jaclyn.
  What's in your chicken nugget? / by Jaclyn Sullivan. — 1st ed.
      p. cm. — (What's in your fast food)
  Includes index.
  ISBN 978-1-4488-6208-5 (library binding) — ISBN 978-1-4488-6375-4 (pbk.) —
  ISBN 978-1-4488-6376-1 (6-pack)
  1. Cooking (Chicken)—Juvenile literature. 2. Convenience foods—Juvenile literature. I. Title.
  TX750.5.C45S85 2012
  641.6'65—dc23
                          2011019554

Manufactured in the United States of America

CPSIA Compliance Information: Batch #WW12PK: For Further Information contact Rosen Publishing, New York, New York at 1-800-237-9932

Contents

Many fast-food restaurants sell chicken nuggets in packs of 4, 5, or 6. Some even sell packs of 10 or 20 nuggets.

Have you ever eaten chicken nuggets? Chicken nuggets are a food many people like to eat. You can buy chicken nuggets at fast-food restaurants. You can also find chicken nuggets at the grocery store. People all around the world enjoy eating chicken nuggets!

Many people think chicken nuggets taste good. Tasting good does not always mean a food is

This girl is using a lot of energy jumping rope. Our bodies are powered by food in much the same way that cars are powered by gas.

good for us, though. Eating too many chicken nuggets can be unhealthy. It is important to eat healthy foods every day. Food gives our bodies **energy**. Energy allows us to do things such as run, jump, and play. We use energy for everything we do!

Nugget Beginnings

A food scientist named Robert Baker invented chicken nuggets in the 1950s. He was trying to think of new ways to use chicken. Baker created a way to form leftover chicken pieces into shapes. He also thought of a way to give the chicken pieces a crispy outside layer, called breading. Baker named his new invention chicken nuggets.

McDonald's sells chicken nuggets all around the world. This McDonald's is in Madrid, Spain.

At first, Baker's nuggets were not very popular. Chicken nuggets looked too different from the chicken people usually ate. Then, in 1983, the fast-food restaurant McDonald's started selling chicken nuggets across the country. Many people tasted these chicken nuggets for the first time and liked them.

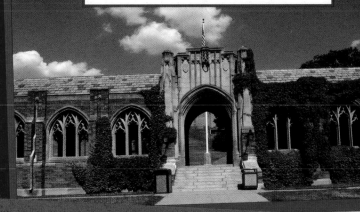

This is Cornell University in Ithaca, New York, where Robert Baker worked from 1957 until 1989. In addition to chicken nuggets, Baker also invented the popular Cornell barbecue sauce.

FAST-FOOD FACTS

Chick-fil-A, a fast-food restaurant, sells more than 1.64 billion chicken nuggets every year. That would be more than 5 nuggets for each person in the United States!

Cool Chickens

As you might guess, chicken nuggets are made from chickens. People in India and Southeast Asia began **domesticating** chickens around 8,000 years ago. Domesticated animals have been raised to live around people. There are now more chickens in the world than any other domesticated bird!

Some chickens are raised to lay eggs. The meat used to make chicken nuggets comes from other

This boy is eating a chicken leg. A chicken leg is also called a drumstick.

chickens raised just for their meat. The kind of chicken most often used for meat is called the Cornish cross. When we talk about chicken meat, we call the legs and thighs of a chicken the dark meat. The chicken breast is called white meat.

In the wild, chickens eat seeds, insects, and lizards. On farms, they are often fed corn and grains.

FAST-FOOD FACTS

Chickens are related to many other birds, such as pheasants and peafowl. Many scientists think they may even be relatives of the Tyrannosaurus rex!

Making Chicken Nuggets

These workers at a chicken-processing plant in China are sorting chicken pieces. Some of this chicken will be mechanically separated and used to make nuggets.

Chicken nuggets are made in factories. Some nuggets are made with white meat. Others are made with **mechanically separated** chicken. This means that machines mash up different parts from different chickens and push them through a **strainer** to take out the bones. Both types of nuggets then have corn and other **ingredients**, like sugar and salt, added in.

Most flour is made from a grain called wheat, seen here. Flour is used in many foods, such as bread, cake, and pasta.

The mixture of chicken and other ingredients is then mashed into a soft paste. Next it is formed into nugget shapes and covered in breading. Some breading is made with bits of dried bread, called breadcrumbs. Other breading is made with flour.

Deep-Frying

After the chicken nuggets are shaped and breaded, they are cooked. Fast-food chicken nuggets are deep-fried. This means they are cooked in hot oil. The hot oil heats the water inside the chicken, which cooks the nugget.

This woman is frying chicken at a fast-food restaurant. The chicken pieces are put in the basket and then lowered into the hot oil to cook.

These chicken nuggets are being deep-fried. Deep-fried foods often have more fat than foods that are baked or grilled.

Deep-frying is not a healthy way to cook. Oil is a form of fat. Some of the fat seeps into the chicken while it cooks. Some natural fat is good for us. Too much added fat can make us sick, though. It makes soft, waxy stuff called **cholesterol** build up in our bodies. Too much cholesterol makes your heart work too hard.

So Much Corn!

Corn is often added to fast-food chicken nuggets. Corn is a grain. It is an important crop to farmers and food makers. It costs a farmer less money to grow corn than to raise chickens. Because it is cheaper, corn is added as

Corn is grown in long, straight rows, as you can see here. Most of the corn grown in the United States is a type of corn called field corn.

FAST-FOOD FACTS

In 2007, the United States grew more than 90 million acres (36 million ha) of corn. Corn is used in many things, from chicken nuggets to plastic cups.

a **filler** to many foods. This means a food maker can use less chicken in chicken nuggets.

Corn is also used to feed chickens. Eating corn makes chickens grow quickly. The faster chickens grow, the sooner they can be used for chicken meat. Sometimes corn is even used in the breading on chicken nuggets. In fact, some chicken nuggets have more corn in them than chicken!

The Extra Stuff

Scientists can create thousands of flavors in labs. These labs are often called flavor factories.

Most fresh food goes bad, or spoils, in about a week. When food spoils, it is not safe to eat. **Preservatives** are added to many foods to stop them from spoiling as quickly. Some preservatives, like salt, are natural. Other preservatives are **artificial**, or manmade. Both natural and artificial preservatives are often added to chicken nuggets.

Artificial flavors and colors are also added to chicken nuggets. Food makers do this because flavors are often lost when foods are **processed**. These added flavors and colors make foods look and taste better. In fact, much of the taste of chicken nuggets comes from these artificial flavors, not the chicken itself!

For many people, artificial ingredients are safe to eat. Some people are allergic to artificial ingredients, though. They might get headaches or rashes from eating them.

Protein Power and Salty Sodium

By itself, chicken can be a very healthy food. Chicken has a lot of a **nutrient** called **protein**. Nutrients are the parts of food that we need to live and grow. Protein helps keep our muscles strong. It even helps our bodies fight diseases.

Chicken nuggets are not as healthy as some other types of cooked chicken, though. They have added sodium, an element found in salt. We need

FAST-FOOD FACTS

Many people dip chicken nuggets in dipping sauces, like ketchup, barbecue sauce, or honey. Dipping sauces can have added sodium though, so look for low-sodium kinds.

some sodium in our **diets**. However, too much sodium is not good for you. It can cause a lot of pressure on the veins that carry blood between your heart and the rest of your body. Over time, this pressure can hurt your heart and kidneys.

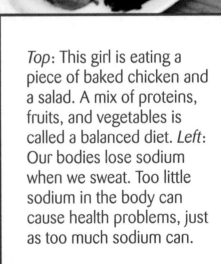

Top: This girl is eating a piece of baked chicken and a salad. A mix of proteins, fruits, and vegetables is called a balanced diet. *Left*: Our bodies lose sodium when we sweat. Too little sodium in the body can cause health problems, just as too much sodium can.

Nutrition Facts

Serving Size 5 Pieces (92g)
Servings Per Container: 50

Amount Per Serving

Calories 260   Calories from Fat 140

	% Daily Value *
Total Fat 16g	25%
Saturated Fat 4g	20%
Trans Fat 0g	
Polyunsaturated Fat 5g	
Monounsaturated Fat 6g	
Cholesterol 75mg	25%
Sodium 450mg	19%
Total Carbohydrate 15g	5%
Dietary Fiber 1g	4%
Sugar 1g	
Protein 14g	28%

Vitamin A 0%	•	Vitamin C 0%
Calcium 4%	•	Iron 6%

*Percent Daily Values are based on a 2,000 calorie diet. Your daily values may be higher or lower depending on your calorie needs.

		Calories	2,000	2,500
Total Fat	Less than		65g	80g
Sat Fat	Less than		20g	25g
Cholesterol	Less than		300mg	300mg
Sodium	Less than		300mg	300mg
Total Carbohydrate			300g	375g
Dietary Fiber			25g	30g

Calories per gram:
Fat 9   •   Carbohydrate 4   •   Protein 4

Check labels to learn more about your food. Labels are usually on the packages that food comes in. They explain what is in food with a list of ingredients. Labels also list nutrition facts. These tell you how much fat, protein, sodium, and other nutrients are in your food.

Labels also tell you how many **calories** are in a serving. Calories measure how much

This is an example of a label on a package of frozen chicken nuggets. The percentages on the right are daily values. You can see that one serving of nuggets gives you 4% of the fiber you should have in one day to stay healthy.

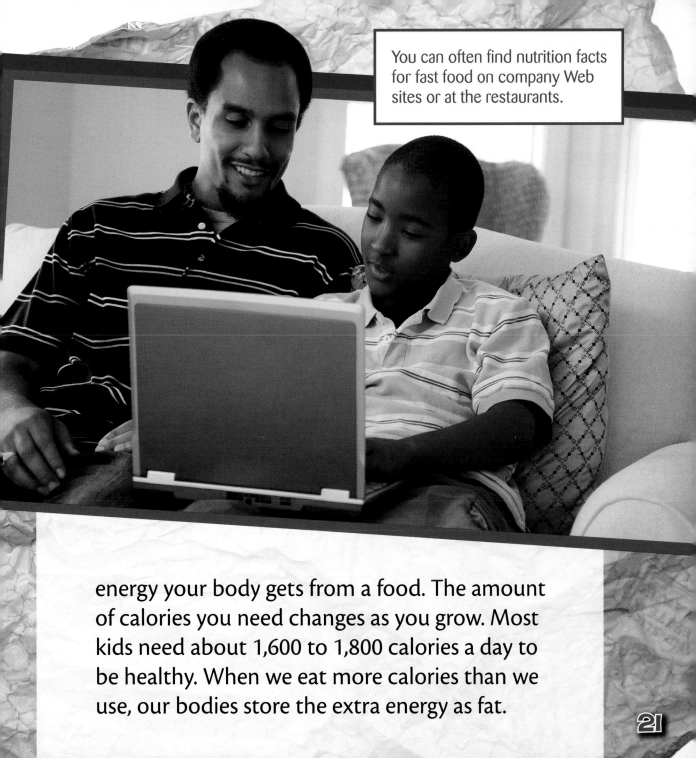

You can often find nutrition facts for fast food on company Web sites or at the restaurants.

energy your body gets from a food. The amount of calories you need changes as you grow. Most kids need about 1,600 to 1,800 calories a day to be healthy. When we eat more calories than we use, our bodies store the extra energy as fat.

Making Healthy Choices

This girl is eating a meal of baked chicken, broccoli, potatoes, and carrots. A meal like this is a healthy choice.

A healthy diet includes lots of different foods, such as fruits and vegetables. Chicken nuggets can be part of a healthy diet if they are eaten only once in a while. Eating too many chicken nuggets can make your body sick, though.

There are many ways to be a healthy eater. When you eat lunch at school, look for grilled or baked chicken instead of fried nuggets. Talk to your parents about making healthy choices at the grocery store. Eating good foods every day will help keep you healthy and strong!

Glossary

artificial (ar-tih-FIH-shul) Made by people, not nature.

calories (KA-luh-reez) Amounts of food that the body uses to keep working.

cholesterol (kuh-LES-teh-rohl) A fatty material that can build up in one's body and increase one's chance of getting heart disease.

diets (DY-uts) Food that people and animals normally eat.

domesticating (duh-MES-tih-kayt-ing) Raising animals to live with people.

energy (EH-ner-jee) The power to work or to act.

filler (FIH-ler) Something used to take up space.

ingredients (in-GREE-dee-unts) The different things that go into food.

mechanically separated (mih-KA-nih-kuh-lee SEH-puh-rayt-ed) Relating to a process in which machines push pieces of meat through a strainer. This separates the bones from the meat that can be eaten.

nutrient (NOO-tree-ent) Food that a living thing needs to live and grow.

preservatives (prih-ZER-vuh-tivz) Substances that keep something from going bad.

processed (PRAH-sesd) Something that is treated or changed using a special series of steps.

protein (PROH-teen) An important element inside the cells of plants and animals.

strainer (STRAYN-ur) Something that sorts out large pieces.

Index

Web Sites

Due to the changing nature of Internet links, PowerKids Press has developed an online list of Web sites related to the subject of this book. This site is updated regularly. Please use this link to access the list:

www.powerkidslinks.com/food/nugget/